This book belongs to

....

The rotten Romans lived long, long ago, and they could be pretty horrible. In this book you will find out all about them – from awful emperors and armies, to foul fights and feasts. There are lots of fun puzzles and pictures to complete with stickers too.

Scholastic Children's Books,
Euston House, 24 Eversholt Street,
London NW1 1DB, UK

A division of Scholastic Ltd
London ~ New York ~ Toronto ~ Sydney ~ Auckland
Mexico City ~ New Delhi ~ Hong Kong

First published in the UK by Scholastic Ltd, 2015

ISBN 978 1407 14372 9

Printed in Malaysia

2 4 6 8 10 9 7 5 3

Terrible Timeline

Read this timeline to find out more about the history of the rotten Romans. Use stickers from the middle of the book to fill in the missing pictures.

START HERE

753 BC
Early Roman farmers live in a place called Latium. This is where the city of Rome was built.

509 BC
The Romans are fed up with their cruel king, Tarquin. They throw him out and rule themselves (that's called a Republic).

264 BC
First of the Punic Wars against Carthage in North Africa. Result: **Rome 1 Carthage 0.**

218 BC
Hannibal of Carthage attacks Rome with elephants. He can't capture Rome but he rampages around Italy terrorising people.

202 BC
Scipio takes charge of the Roman Army and beats Hannibal. Result: **Rome 2 Carthage 0.**

146 BC
Carthage is wiped out completely.

AD 60
One tribe in Britain, the Iceni, rebel. Queen Boudica leads them in battle against the Romans and kills thousands of them. Then she is defeated and she poisons herself.

AD 80
Julius Agricola completes the invasion of Britain (except for the Picts in Scotland).

AD 43
Claudius gives orders for the invasion of Britain ... again!

AD 122
Hadrian starts building a wall across northern England to keep out the Picts.

44 BC
Julius Caesar is elected dictator for life – then murdered!

AD 235–285
Fifty-year period with over twenty Roman emperors, mainly because they keep getting murdered.

AD 401
Roman troops are withdrawn from Britain to defend Rome from attack.

55 BC
Julius Caesar invades Britain for the first time for the country's tin, copper and lead.

AD 1453
End of the Roman Empire.

Roman Rulers

The Romans got through a lot of loathsome leaders. They often only reigned for a short time because they kept getting murdered. Here are some facts about the foulest ones.

EMPEROR CALIGULA

RULED: AD 37–41

FAVOURITE SAYING: "Rome is a city of necks just waiting for me to chop."

DAFTEST ACT: Making his favourite horse a consul so it could help rule the empire.

STICKY END: One of his trusted guards stabbed him to death.

EMPEROR TIBERIUS

RULED: AD 14–37

FAVOURITE SAYING: "I don't care if they hate me ... as long as they obey me."

NASTIEST HABIT: Breaking the legs of anyone who disobeyed him.

STICKY END: He died aged 78, probably suffocated by his chief helper. Everyone had a big party once he was gone!

EMPEROR NERO

RULED: AD 54–68

FAVOURITE SAYING: He played the lyre very badly. When he knew he was going to die he said "What a loss I shall be to the art of music!"

NASTIEST HABIT: Murdering people. Nero killed his half brother, his wife, his girlfriend, and his mother too!

STICKY END: He knew he was about to be arrested, so he asked one of his men to cut his throat.

EMPEROR CLAUDIUS

RULED: AD 41–54

FAVOURITE SAYING: "I'm sorry I get so angry, but I can't help it. I just love killing people so much!"

NASTIEST HABIT: Watching criminals being tortured.

STICKY END: His niece, Agrippina, poisoned him with mushrooms.

Cruel Julius

Julius Caesar was one of the greatest Roman rulers, but he got too big for his boots, so he was murdered ... by his friend! Read his story to find out more about his dreadful death, then colour in the picture on the page opposite.

Lots of people thought that Julius Caesar wanted to be "King of the Romans". The last time the Romans had had a king in charge, things had gone very wrong indeed, so they didn't want Caesar to make the same mistakes. Something had to be done.

Caesar was due to speak at the Senate (the Roman parliament) on 15 March 44 BC. His killers decided this would be the best time to murder him.

There were lots of signs to warn Caesar about going to the Senate – a fortune teller told him not to go, his wife begged him to stay at home after having strange dreams, and even Caesar himself awoke on the 15 March feeling almost too ill to make his speech. None of this was enough to stop him from going.

When Caesar entered the Senate, the senators all stood up as a sign of respect. Some members of the gang of killers slipped behind his chair, and one of them pulled Caesar's robe from around his neck. This was the signal for the attack.

Each of the killers took a dagger and stabbed Caesar. He fought back bravely, but he was not strong enough, and he died with 23 stab wounds all over his body.

Awesome Army

The Romans were fearsome warriors and they were famous for their well-organised and deadly army.

Read these facts about the Roman army and its savage soldiers and mark each one with a sticker if you think it's true, and a sticker if you think it's false. You can find the answers on page 32.

I. If you joined the Roman army you would have to stay in it for 25 years.

2. The emperor paid for the soldiers' uniforms, weapons, food and burial.

3. The punishment for laziness in the army was to be forced to sleep outside the safety of the camp.

4. Soldiers in the Roman army were not allowed to get married.

5. If you were the first soldier over the wall of an enemy town, you would be rewarded with a medal and a feast in your honour.

6. If you were part of a town conquered by the Romans and you didn't want to join the Roman army you didn't have to.

7. You weren't allowed to be a soldier unless you were more than 180cm tall.

8. Instead of toilet paper, the Roman soldiers would use a sponge on a stick.

Dress Up Rattus

Use stickers from the middle of the book to make Rattus look his awful best.

Soldier

Emperor

Foul Roman Feasts

The rotten Romans loved their food, and would often have large feasts and banquets where lots of truly foul food was served. Here are some food facts to make your mouth water or maybe turn your stomach...

During some feasts, guests would eat so much that they would make themselves sick... and then they'd keep right on eating!

Emperor Maximinus Thrax was a big eater. He was supposed to have eaten 20 kilograms of meat a day.

The Romans had some sickly sauces. One was made from rotting fish guts, which the Romans would add to their meals a bit like you use tomato ketchup today.

Emperor Elagabalus once served his guests peas mixed with grains of gold and lentils mixed with jewels.

The Emperor is having a banquet but the menu has got a bit muddled up. Each letter has jumped on two places in the alphabet. Can you work out what's for dinner?

Answers are on page 32.

1. Uvwhhgf fqtokeg

....

2. Upcknu kp oknm

....

3. Quvtkej dtckpu

....

4. Uvgygf ugcyggf

....

5. Hncokpiq vqpiwg rkg

....

6. Ecogn jggnu

Spot The Lot

Gory Gladiators

The rotten Romans loved a good fight. Thousands of people would come to arenas to watch gladiators fighting with swords and spears. Sometimes they battled each other, and sometimes they were up against wild animals. Here are some facts about these truly savage sports...

• Sometimes it wasn't even the fighters who ended up injured. At an arena in Pompeii, rioting broke out in the audience, and lots of people died!

• If a gladiator gave up during a fight he could surrender. The emperor would then decide if he deserved to live or not. Thumbs up meant life, thumbs down meant death.

• In one very, very gruesome day in AD 80, 5,000 animals were killed in one arena in Rome.

I THINK IT'S FULL

Terrible Timeline p2-3

Dress Up Rattus p10-11

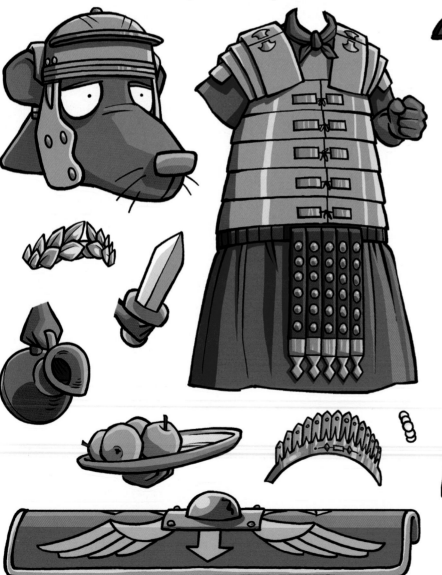   

Dress Up Rattus p10-11

Gladiator Shield p17

Where's Rattus? p18-19

Dress Up Rattus p22-23

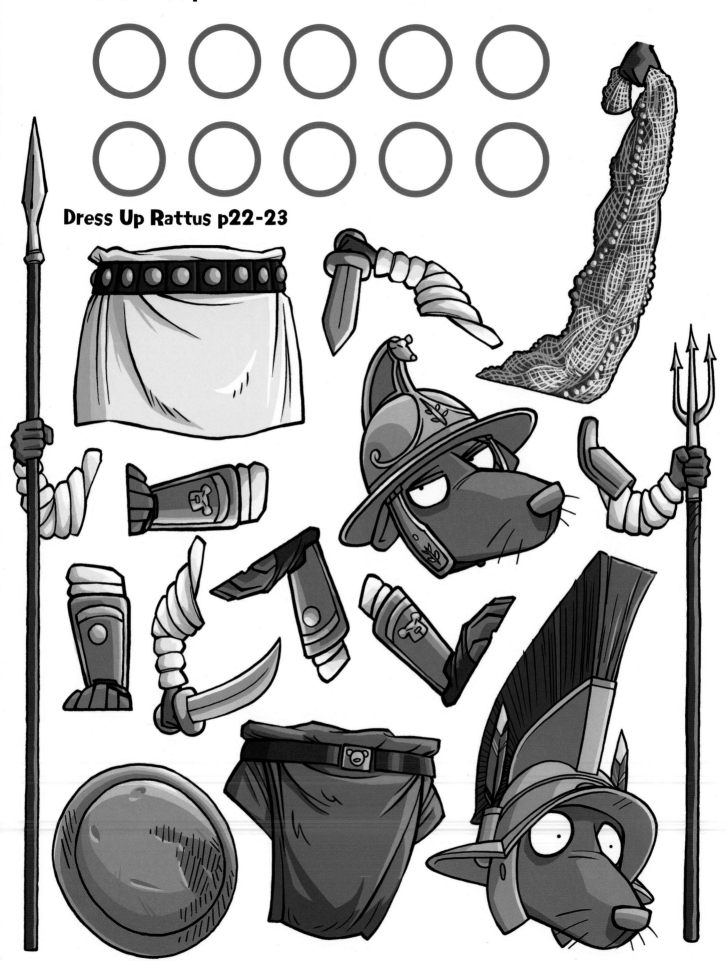

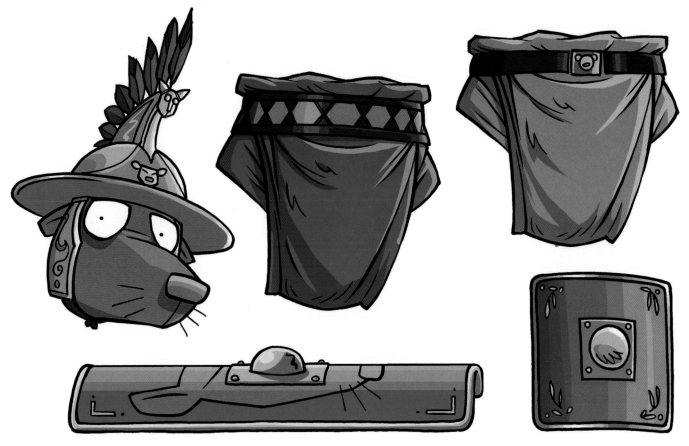

What Did They Do For Us? p26

COMPUTER GAMES	CALENDARS	FIREMEN
PUBLIC LIBRARIES	KARAOKE	ICE HOCKEY
CENTRAL HEATING	SANDWICHES	SEWERS
STAMPS	BIKINIS	FALSE TEETH

Awesome Arena p30-31

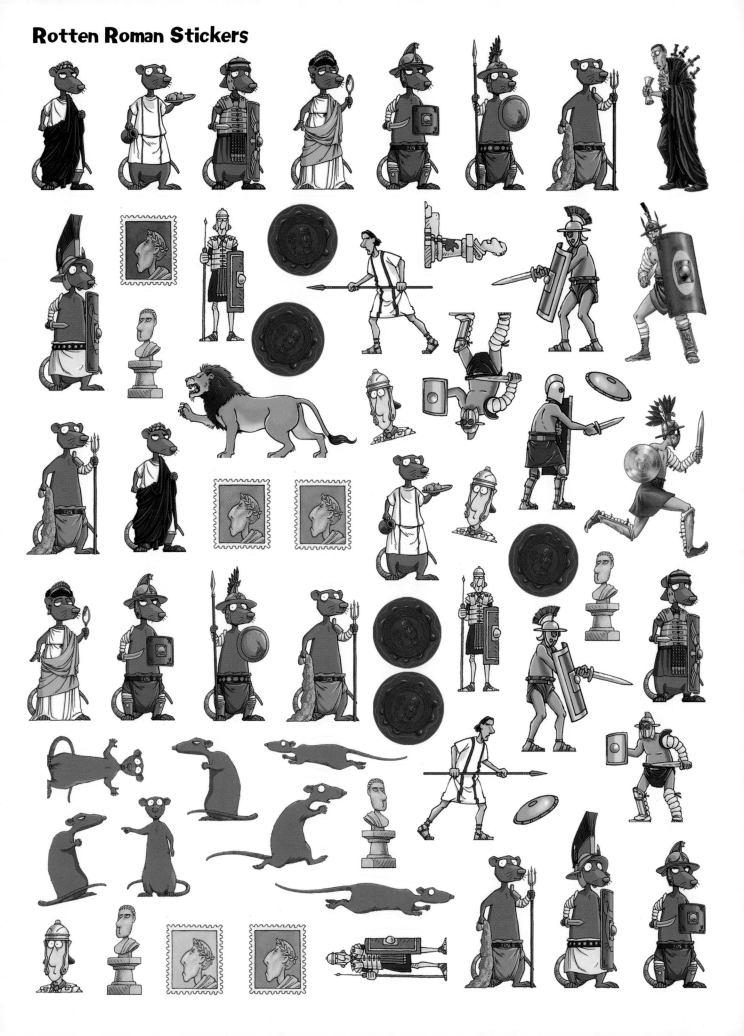

Rotten Roman Stickers

Use stickers from the middle of the book to decorate this gladiator's shield.

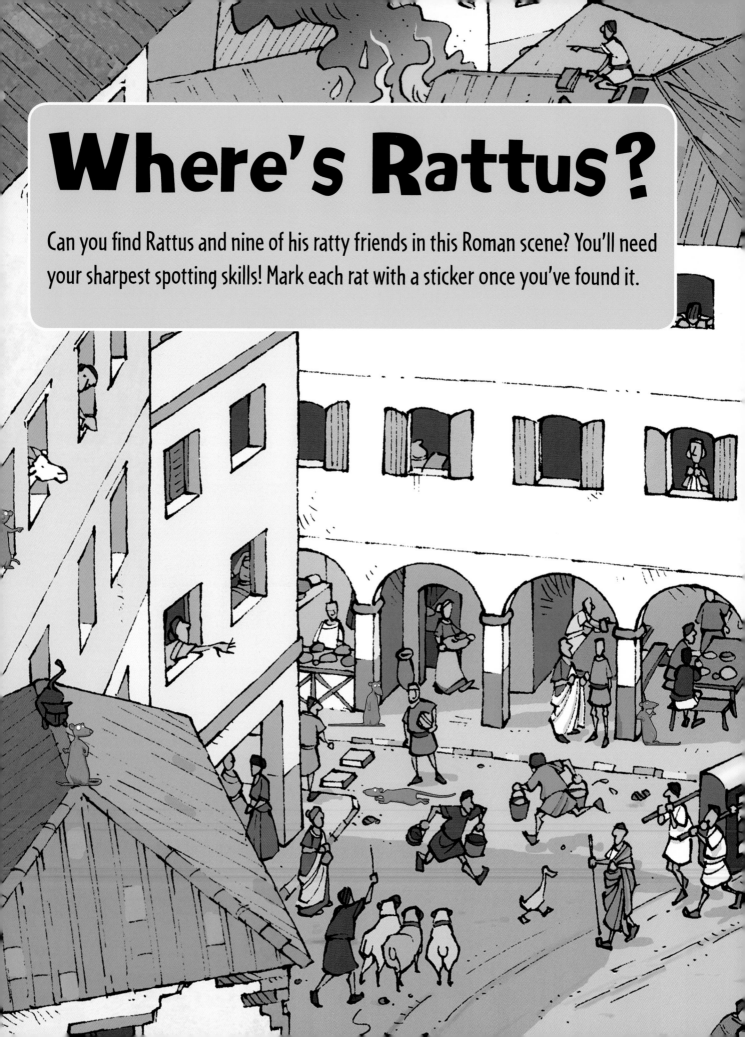

Where's Rattus?

Can you find Rattus and nine of his ratty friends in this Roman scene? You'll need your sharpest spotting skills! Mark each rat with a sticker once you've found it.

Rotten Roman Fun and Games

Roman children's games were a bit like ours are today. Here are some that you might want to try with your friends...

Trigon

What You Need:

• Two friends to play with
• Three inflated pig's bladders (if you don't have bladders available, you can use three tennis balls instead)
• Chalk

How To Play:

1. Draw a triangle on the playground with chalk, with sides about 2 metres long.

2. One player stands at each corner of the triangle.

3. Start with one bladder/ball and pass it between you. The aim of the game is to keep it in the air for as long as possible.

4. Sounds easy, right? Now add the other two balls so each player has one. There is no set order for passing the ball, so you may have to pass your ball while catching two from the other players!

5. The winner is the one who drops the ball the fewest number of times.

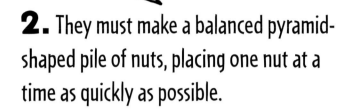

Nuts

What You Need:

• A supply of nuts, ideally hazelnuts
• Some friends to play with

How To Play:

1. Each player takes an equal number of nuts.

2. They must make a balanced pyramid-shaped pile of nuts, placing one nut at a time as quickly as possible.

3. The winner is the player who uses the most nuts before the pyramid collapses.

(**Note:** This is a game for children. When you grew up, the Romans would say you had "left your nuts".)

Dress Up Rattus

Dress Rattus like the gory gladiators of ancient Rome, and get him ready for action!

Incredible Invaders

The Roman army were excellent fighters, and they wanted to take over as much land as possible. When they came to Britain, though, they had a real fight on their hands. Here are some foul facts about the most brutal battles.

INVASION TAKE 1

Vercingetorix v. Caesar

Emperor Julius Caesar invades Britain for the first time. Celtic chief Vercingetorix tries to stop Caesar and his Roman army from getting into the capital city by building a stone wall with a ditch around it. Caesar builds towers on wheels to push up to the walls and climb over. Vercingetorix builds an even taller tower behind the walls and throws fireballs on top of the Romans. The Romans catch hold of the top of the wall with hooks, and climb up ropes attached to them. But Vercingetorix pulls the hooks up and drags them inside the city. During the Roman attack it begins to rain heavily. The Celtic defenders run for shelter and hope the Romans will do the same. The Romans keep going, and begin to kill every man, woman and child in sight. Vercingetorix orders his best fighting men to escape through a back entrance.

Result: Caesar wins!

INVASION TAKE 2

Boudica v. Claudius

Emperor Claudius give orders for the invasion of Britain... again! One tribe in Britain, the Iceni, rebel.

Their leader is Queen Boudica. She leads them in battle against the Romans and kills thousands of them. Although her name means 'Victory', she is defeated and poisons herself.

Result: Claudius wins!

INVASION TAKE 3

Hadrian v. the Picts

Everyone in Britain is defeated, apart from the Picts in Scotland. Emperor Hadrian starts building a wall across northern England to keep the Picts out. (But they still get in!)

Result: The Romans eventually withdraw from Britain because they need to go home and defend Rome.

25

What Did They Do For Us?

The rotten Romans ran the world for a long time. There are still signs of their life around today. You probably use things the Romans invented every day, without even knowing it. Find the word stickers in the middle of the book and decide if you think each one is a Roman invention. Stick it in the 'True' column if you think it is, and the 'False' column if you think it's not.

True

False

As well as useful inventions, there are some rotten things in Britain today that we can blame the Romans for. They brought them here. Things like...

stinging nettles - next time you sit on one, you can cry out in agony, "Oooh! The rotten Romans!"

cabbages and peas - the sort of vegetables your parents make you eat because "they're good for you." Next time you hear that, you can say, "The Ancient Britons lived for a few million years without them, so I can too!"

cats - yes, blame the Romans for that mangy moggy that yowls all night on the corner of your street and keeps you awake. When teacher tells you off for yawning in class, say, "Don't blame me - blame the rotten Romans!"

rotten spelling - a lot of the words we use today come from Latin. They made sense to the rotten Romans but they don't make sense to us. Take the Latin word "plumbum"... no, it doesn't mean purple bottom. It means waterworks. So we get a word for a man who fixes your leaky waterworks from that. That's right, "plumber". Next time you get two out of ten for your spelling test say, "Don't blame me - blame the rotten Romans!"

Cruel Quiz

Take this quiz to find out how much you really know about the rotten Romans.
The answers are on page 32.

1. Roman children used a bit of a pig as a ball. Which bit did they use?

A) The snout
B) The stomach
C) The lungs

2. What was the punishment in court for murdering your wife because she drank wine?

A) No punishment
B) Being beaten to death
C) Being set on fire

3. What did the Romans use as toothpaste?

A) Wine
B) Powdered mouse brains
C) Crushed-up rubies

4. In Roman horse races, what happened to the winning horse?

A) It was given a medal
B) It was presented to the emperor as a gift
C) It was killed as a sacrifice

5. What was strange about the Roman god, Janus?

A) He was a giant
B) He had huge fangs
C) He had two faces

6. Emperor Caligula's real name was Gaius. Caligula was just his nickname, but what did it mean?

A) Great King
B) Little Boot
C) Big Bear

Awesome Arena

Fill the arena with gladiators, savage beasts and more rotten Roman chaos using stickers from the middle of the book.

MAIN EVENTS
MORNING
ANIMAL HUNTS
LUNCHTIME
EXECUTIONS
AFTERNOON
GLADIATORS

All the Horrible Answers

Awesome Army p8-9

1. TRUE
2. FALSE – you had to pay for them yourself
3. TRUE
4. TRUE
5. FALSE – you would be given a crown made of gold
6. FALSE – you had to join or you would be sentenced to death
7. FALSE – you could be between 1.6m and 1.8m tall
8. TRUE

Foul Feasts p12-13

1. Stuffed dormice
2. Snails in milk
3. Ostrich brains
4. Stewed seaweed
5. Flamingo tongue pie
6. Camel heels

What Did They Do For Us? p26-27

TRUE:	FALSE:
Sewers	Karaoke
Public Libraries	Computer Games
Calendars	Stamps
Central Heating	Sandwiches
False Teeth	Bikinis
Firemen	Ice Hockey

Spot The Lot p14-15

IT'S THE ELEPHANT OF SURPRISE

Where's Rattus? p18-19

Cruel Quiz p28-29   1.B, 2.A, 3.B, 4.C, 5.C, 6.B